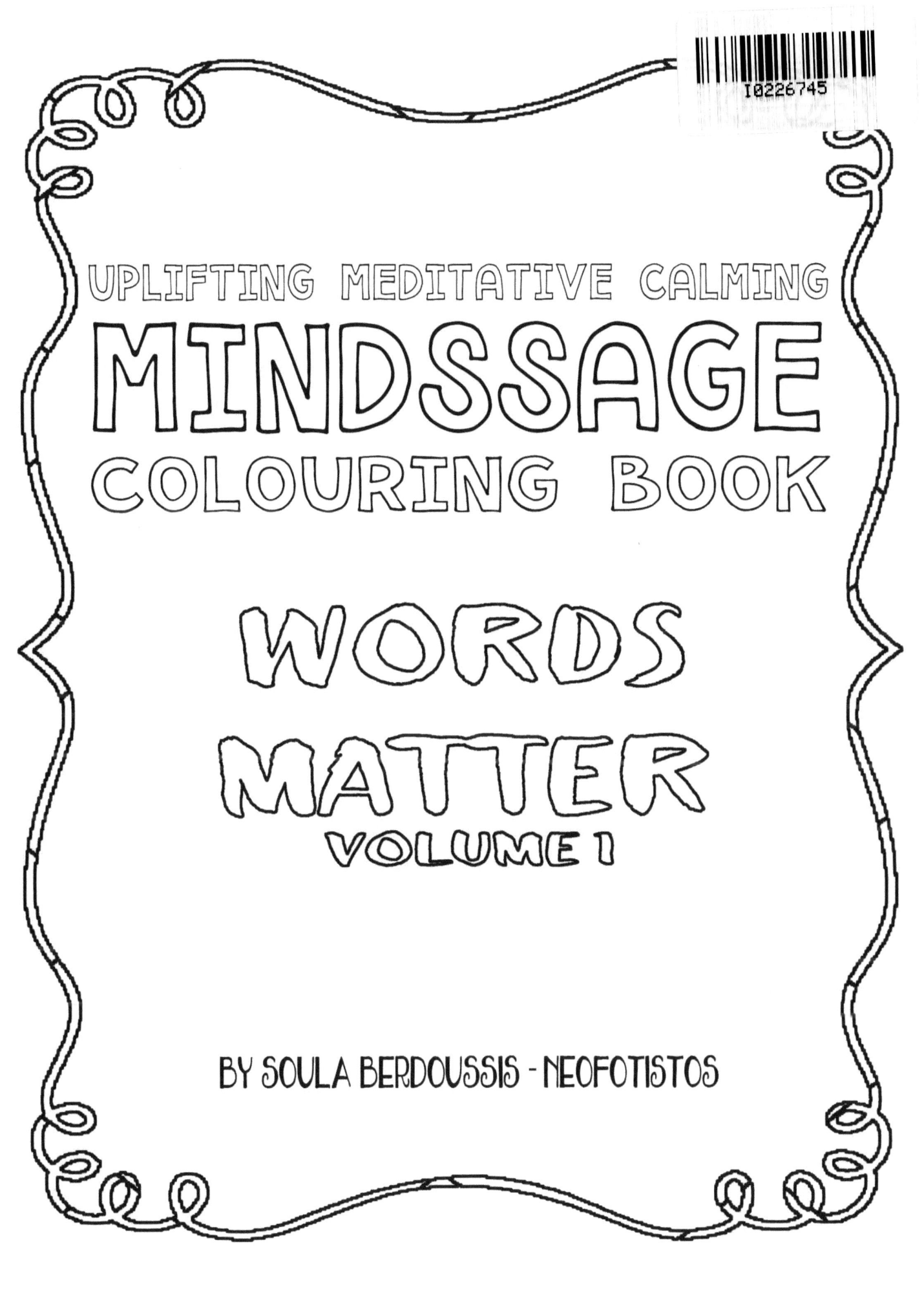

Copyright © 2016 Soula Neofotistos
All rights reserved. No part of this publication may be stored, reproduced, distributed, or transmitted in any form or by any means, including photocopying, recording, or other electronic or mechanical methods, without the prior written permission of the publisher.
ISBN: 978-0-9953362-0-9
Printed in the United States of America
Created and Published by Soula Neofotistos
First Edition - Volume 1
www.mindssagecolouringbooks.com

This series was created with the purpose of promoting effective communication and building self-esteem and confidence. All while people of all ages enjoy a wonderful, creative doodle and colouring pastime.

Imagine being inspired by beautifully chosen uplifting, meditative and calming positive words to colour. MINDSSAGE Colouring Book series provides just that! As an EFT Life Coach and Creator of the Mindssage Colouring Book series, I have combined my knowledge of the importance of the words you choose and the way you use them with a practice of mindfulness through colouring. The repetition of the positive and enlightening words on each colouring page is all you need to start to attract a more positive experience of life. And you will discover the creative colourist that you are.

It's a whole new colouring world with words
-There aren't any rules. You can colour inside the lines, outside the lines, in one colour or in dozens of colours.
-You can do candy cane-colouring, halfsies-colouring, and bubble gum-colouring (see website).

Benefits of Colouring

- memory improvement
- de stressing
- expressing yourself
- developing your focusing skills
- personal creativity
- developing your mindfulness skills
- massaging and relaxing the mind

What is: "Doodle Dee and Doodle Lou" page? Doodling is an extension of your imagination where you allow your inner greatness to come to life on a piece of paper.

Simply put, this is YOUR time and YOU decide what to doodle and what to colour.

So... choose your favourite spot, grab your MINDSSAGE Colouring Book, pick your favourite colouring pencils, unplug all digital devices and start the fun!

DOODLE DEE AND DOODLE LOU

LOVE... is at the root of all creation

DOODLE DEE AND DOODLE LOU

EXCITED... the feeling from within

DOODLE DEE AND DOODLE LOU

HARMONY... uniting peacefully

DOODLE DEE AND DOODLE LOU

PEACEFUL... times of peace

DOODLE DEE AND DOODLE LOU

LIVING... a daily nourishment

DOODLE DEE AND DOODLE LOU

LIFE... life will always continue

DOODLE DEE AND DOODLE LOU

GROWTH... a magical process

DOODLE DEE AND DOODLE LOU

VISIONARY... you see it now... what will be

DOODLE DEE AND DOODLE LOU

TRANSFORMATION... be the change you would like to see

DOODLE DEE AND DOODLE LOU

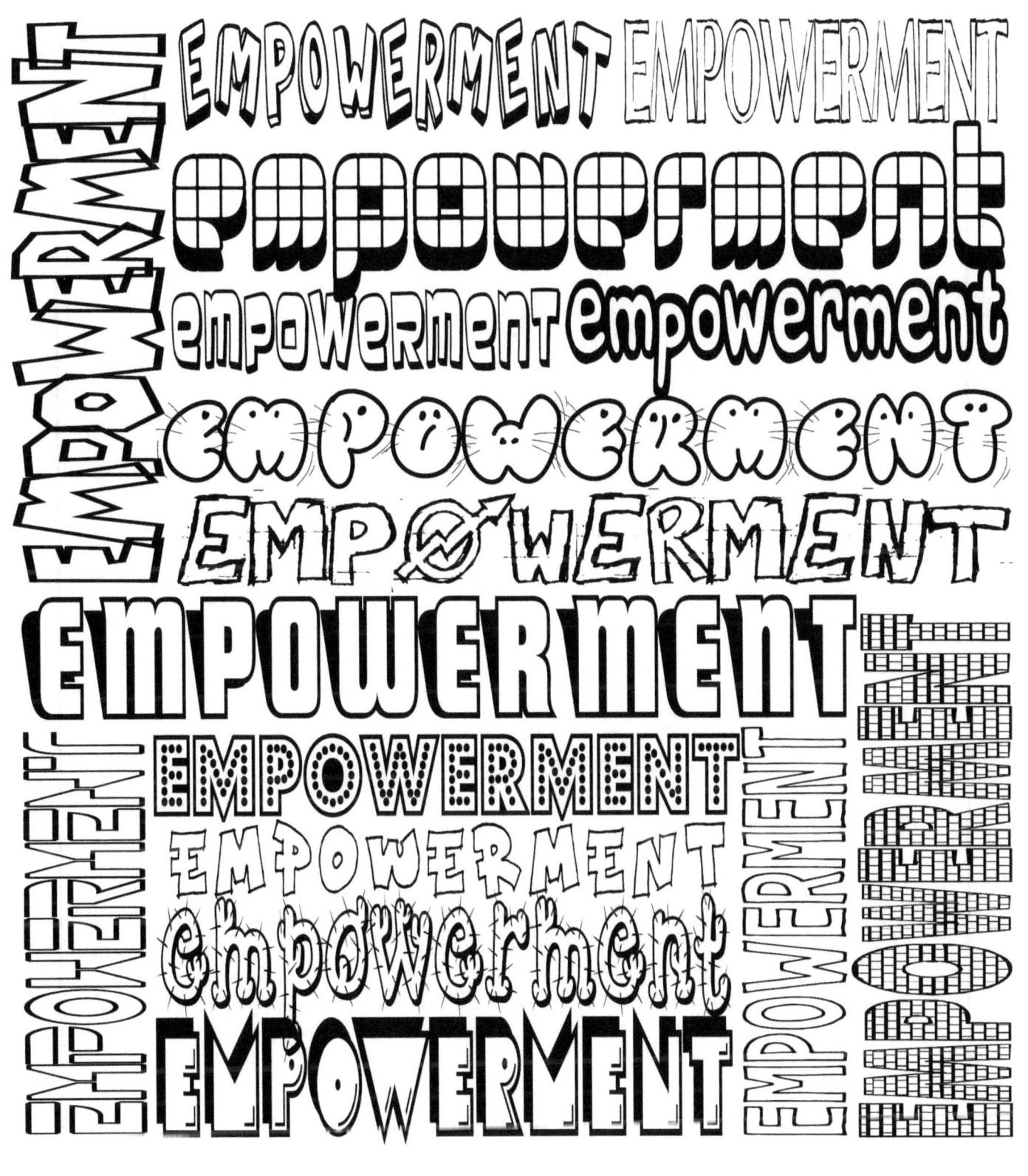

EMPOWERMENT... understand the power is in you and always has been - find it

DOODLE DEE AND DOODLE LOU

GRACE... stand up and be present

DOODLE DEE AND DOODLE LOU

ACCEPT... recognize and be aware of what is true

DOODLE DEE AND DOODLE LOU

FUN... look around... the amusement can be heard and felt everywhere

DOODLE DEE AND DOODLE LOU

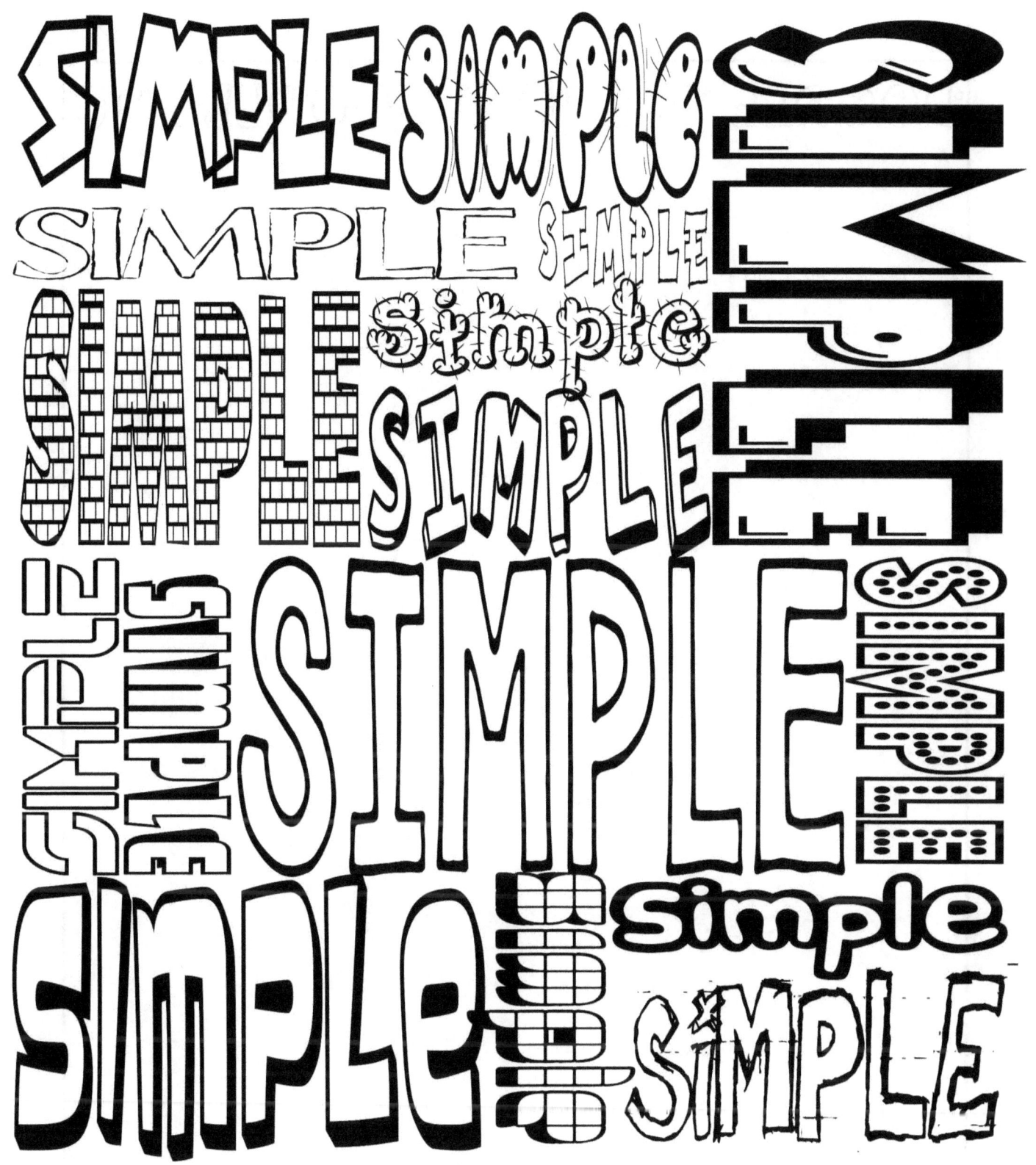

SIMPLE... easily understood with no difficulty

DOODLE DEE AND DOODLE LOU

MIDNFULNESS... try living in the "NOW"

DOODLE DEE AND DOODLE LOU

LAUGHTER... sound of amusement coming from the heart

DOODLE DEE AND DOODLE LOU

THINK... think about it for a minute... think... think.... think!

DOODLE DEE AND DOODLE LOU

HAPPY... a pleasure to be around

DOODLE DEE AND DOODLE LOU

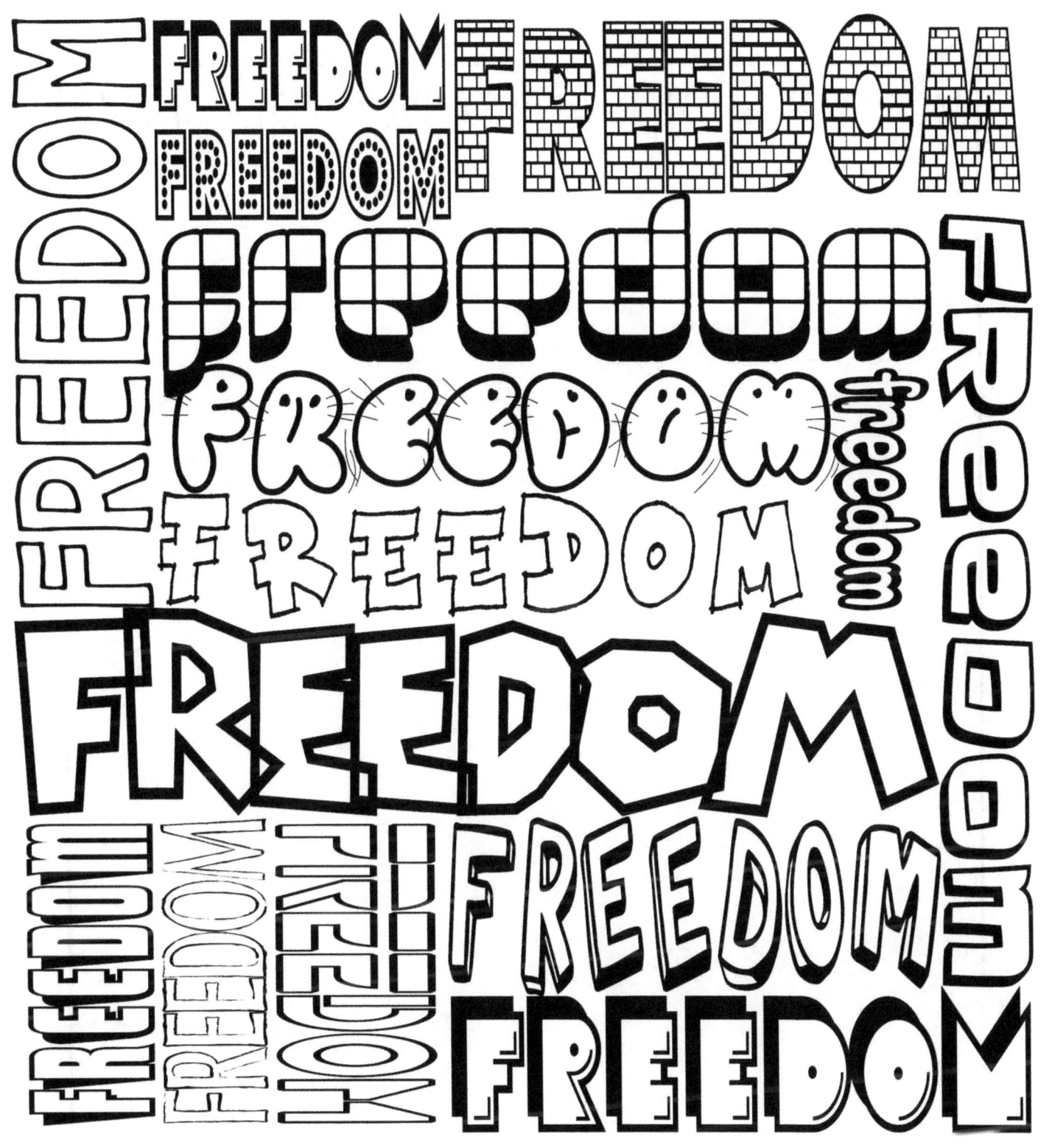

FREEDOM... flying like a bird

DOODLE DEE AND DOODLE LOU

FOCUS... where your interests are

DOODLE DEE AND DOODLE LOU

CLARITY

CLARITY... particularly clear about what I am doing

DOODLE DEE AND DOODLE LOU

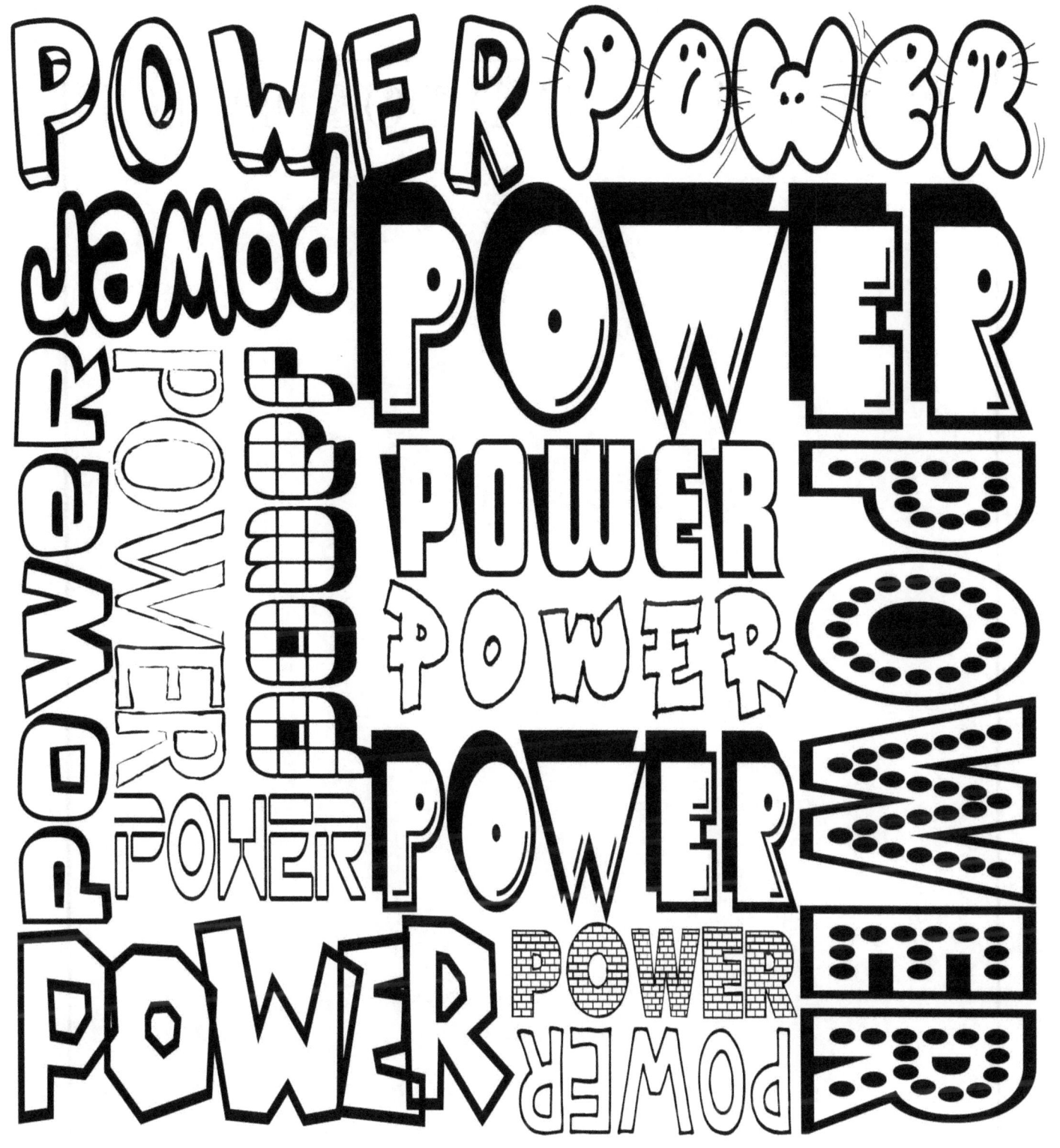

POWER... direct or influence in the right way

DOODLE DEE AND DOODLE LOU

BLISS... reaching a state of perfect happiness

DOODLE DEE AND DOODLE LOU

FORGIVE... set yourself free

DOODLE DEE AND DOODLE LOU

DREAM... floating thoughts, images, and emotions

DOODLE DEE AND DOODLE LOU

PLAYING... take part

DOODLE DEE AND DOODLE LOU

DECIDE... make up your mind

DOODLE DEE AND DOODLE LOU

LEADER... builder of sorts

DOODLE DEE AND DOODLE LOU

AMBITIOUS... live the dream

DOODLE DEE AND DOODLE LOU

SUNSHINE... brightens the world

DOODLE DEE AND DOODLE LOU

EFFECTIVE... see yourself putting one foot in front of the other

DOODLE DEE AND DOODLE LOU

MEDITATION... preparing to clear things out

DOODLE DEE AND DOODLE LOU

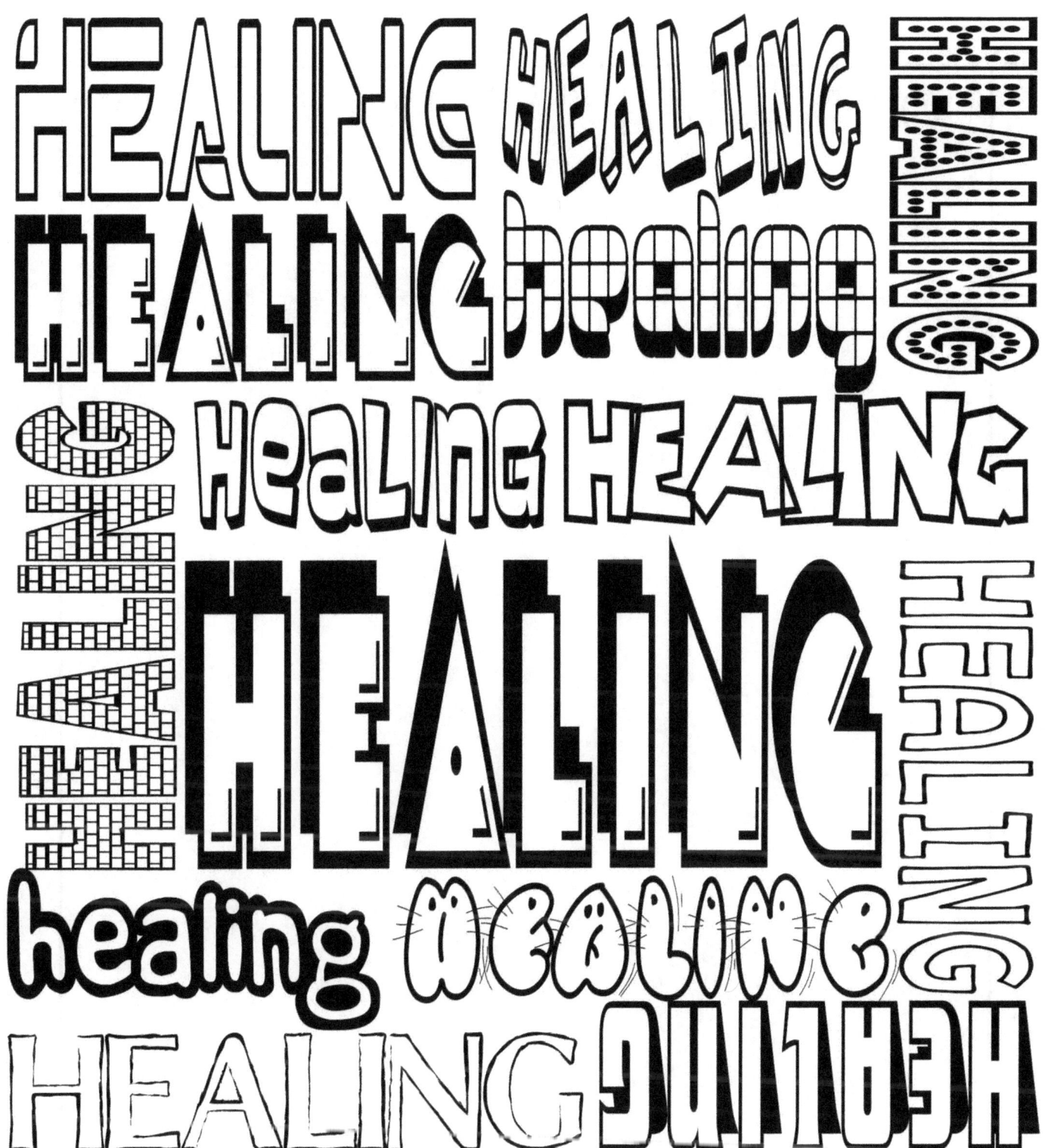

HEALING... everything is new and wonderful

DOODLE DEE AND DOODLE LOU

ENCOURAGE... sparkle and grow

DOODLE DEE AND DOODLE LOU

DOODLE DEE AND DOODLE LOU

INSPIRE... filling up with vision

DOODLE DEE AND DOODLE LOU

TERRIFIC... awesome... great... good

DOODLE DEE AND DOODLE LOU

SPECIAL... different than the usual

DOODLE DEE AND DOODLE LOU

CREATE... sowing the seeds

DOODLE DEE AND DOODLE LOU

ENGAGE... getting involved is so much fun

DOODLE DEE AND DOODLE LOU

ABUNDANCE... overflowing and keep it coming

DOODLE DEE AND DOODLE LOU

THANKFUL... it all worked out just like I thought

DOODLE DEE AND DOODLE LOU

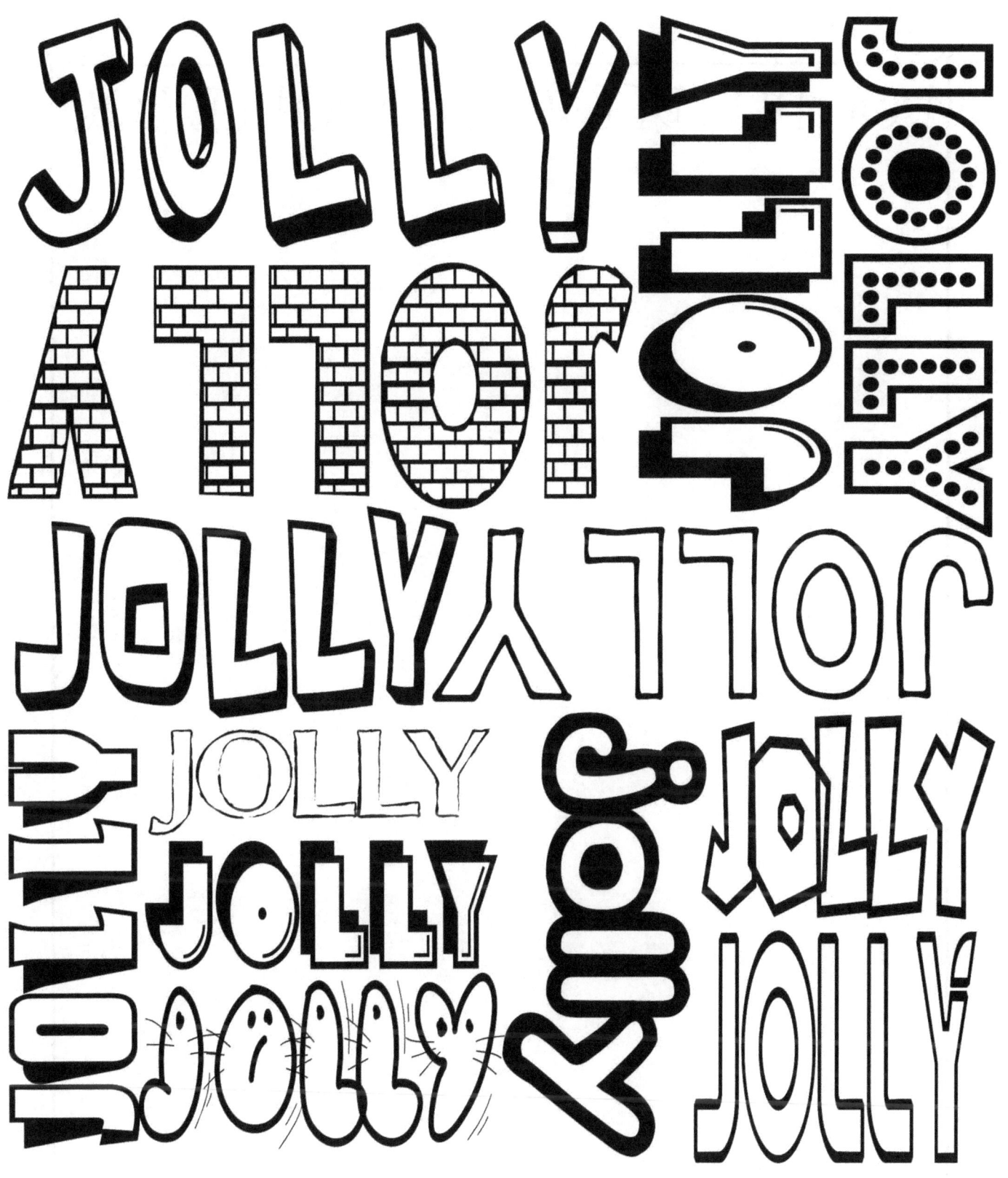

JOLLY... full abundance of cheer

DOODLE DEE AND DOODLE LOU

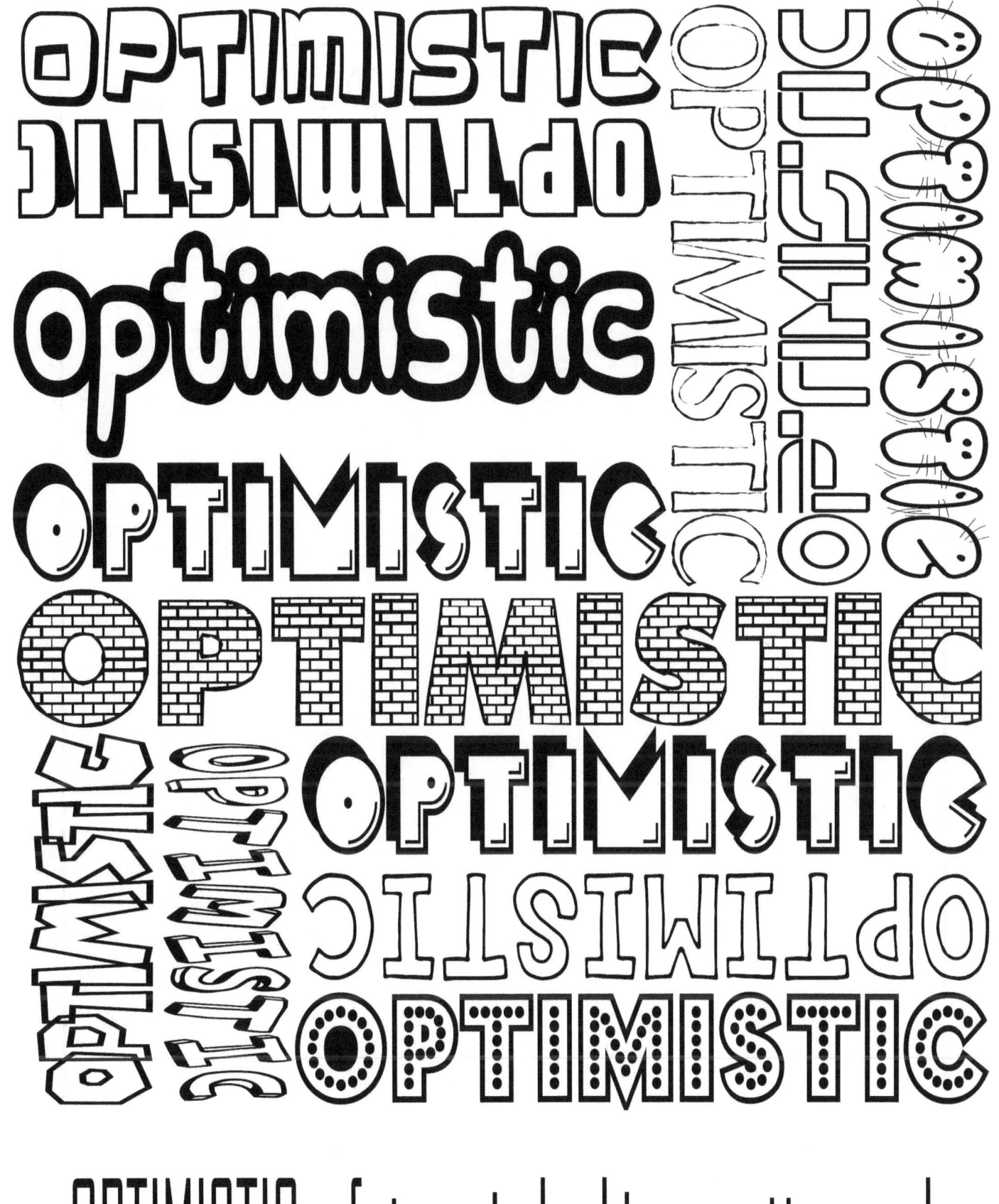

OPTIMISTIC... future is looking pretty good

DOODLE DEE AND DOODLE LOU

DELIGHTFUL... pleasantly pleasant

DOODLE DEE AND DOODLE LOU

ENERGY... the power source for all

DOODLE DEE AND DOODLE LOU

SMILE... brightens up the face

DOODLE DEE AND DOODLE LOU

IMAGINE... seeing is believing

DOODLE DEE AND DOODLE LOU

TITLES AVAILABLE

WORDS MATTER

I AM MATTERS

CONFIDENCE MATTERS

INSPIRATION MATTERS

COMING SOON

WORDS MATTER II

BIBLE WORDS MATTER

THINKING MATTERS

REMEMBER A GOOD TIME MATTERS

TAKING A BREAK MATTERS

ASKING YOURSELF MATTERS

ASKING YOURSELF MATTERS II

www.ingramcontent.com/pod-product-compliance
Lightning Source LLC
LaVergne TN
LVHW061314060426
835507LV00019B/2155